MW01133592

"Michelle's book is a beautiful masterpiece and a 'must have' for every parent and educator, or any other person who loves children and wants to protect them. This fast-paced, page tuner has a magical style that will immediately engage young and old in a topic that is crying out for attention. Michelle masterfully uses humor and her amazing imagination to make it safe enough to look at how cruelty can breed shame, fear and isolation in all of us. Readers will be delighted to consider the different creative options to respond to bullying throughout the book and engage in a practical, step-by-step road map at the end of the book to engage in a dialogue that will transform one's view of bullying into one of compassion. Most importantly, 'Hey Loser, What's for lunch?' will give children AND adults a path leading towards safety, forgiveness, and healing."

—JOHN P. WALKER PH.D, LMFT

HEY LOSER,
WHAT'S FOR LUNCH?

HEY LOSER, WHAT'S FOR LUNCH?

Breaking the cycle of bullying
by identifying bullying and opening up
the lines of communication

MICHELLE BARBIERI

Clovercroft Publishing

Hey Loser, What's for Lunch?

©2018 by Michelle Barbieri

All rights reserved. No part of this book may be reproduced or transmitted in any form or by any means, electronic or mechanical, including photocopying, recording or by any information storage and retrieval system, without permission in writing from the copyright owner.

Published by Clovercroft Publishing, Franklin, Tennessee

Published in association with Larry Carpenter of Christian Book Services, LLC
www.christianbookservices.com

Edited by Tammy Kling and Tiarra Tompkins

Cover and Interior Design by Suzanne Lawing

Cover Illustration by Deena Su Oteh

Printed in the United States of America

ISBN: 978-1-945507-83-0

HeyLoserWhatsForLunch.com

DEDICATION

I would like to thank my boys, Orion and Brooks, who I love more than anything in the universe times infinity. You are my world and my world is perfect because of you. I am so very proud of you both. You will always be mommies shining stars. Who will take on the world, head on, and not be afraid to change your stars. Always remember, without failure there is no success. Life's failures and painful moments are learning experiences that will strengthen and empower you to change not only your own life but make a positive difference in others' lives. Don't be afraid to stand out and be unique. Always be you and not what you think others want you to be or tell you to be. Most importantly, never be silenced by a bully no matter who they may be. Speak up and let your voice be heard.

ACKNOWLEDGEMENTS

There are not enough words of thanks for my editors at OnFire Books. Their guidance and encouragement gave wings to my dream of helping others. My book would not be what it is today without their support and wisdom.

Thank you to my publisher Larry Carpenter and his team. His expertise in the publishing world helped guide me on every aspect on being successful in publishing my book.

Thank you to my Illustrator Deena So'Oteh for her exceptional front cover illustration. Deena took a written concept and breathed life into it by creating an image that needs no words to evoke an emotion from all ages.

Without these invaluable people, my book wouldn't have been possible. It would be a dusty manuscript sitting in the drawer of an antique wooden railway station desk, a dream without wings.

CONTENTS

INTRODUCTION

Bullying is a serious epidemic that affects everyone at some point in their life. Bullying ranges from moderate to severe with the bully utilizing words, emotions and/or physical abuse as their weapon to take control over their victims. Bullying does not discriminate and can have as early onset as the age of four. It's extremely important for us to continue to reach out to our children to try and prevent them from being bullied and to help them from becoming bullies. If there was ever a cause to never give up on changing, bullying is it. Our children deserve nothing less from their parents, teachers and care takers. Children and adults are dying, every day, at the hands of bullies. Mass murders have become more of a horrific event in every country. We are becoming more and more divided. Where we should be coming together as a united front. Children are part of the 1st step to helping change the world. For the bullies we ignore and cultivate today will only grow to become the monsters we fear in the future.

I myself have been bullied at different stages in my life from childhood and in my adult life. It sadly ranged from moderate to severe involving verbal, emotional and physical abuse. I initially started writing this book, years ago, when my eldest was four years old. When something happens to you, you deal and life goes on but when something happens to your child, the world stops. One day, he came home from pre-k with bruises on his forehead. At first, he was very quiet and reluctant to tell me what happened. Through love and support, he opened up to me that evening. It turns out; it was two boys, his age, kicking him in the head with their shoes on the playground. As we talked, it came to light this was not the first incident and they were bullying other children in his class as well. This was the tipping of the scales and when I decided enough is enough. I wanted to make a difference in this world and help others not become a victim like my son and myself. I wanted to break the cycle and help not only the victims but also the bullies. Bullying is a cry for help. That cry is different for each bully but none the less it's a cry. I wrote this book to help identify children who were being bullied and help get them the help they need before it's too late. Help us stop bulling on our playgrounds and in our lives. Someone you know or maybe it's you who is being bullied at this moment, or has been bullied at some point in their life. Step up and lend a helping hand to stop an abusive one. Help us identify the victims and the bullies and get help for all involved before it's too late.

The second part of this book is meant to bring to light helpful information about bullying and on how to identify if your child is a victim or a bully. It's also to help assist parents in opening up the lines of communication with their children. This is a brief discovery stage and not an in depth knowledge based book. The author is not a trained professional. For further assistance, beyond the pages of this book, please seek the assistance of a trained professional if your child is being bullied, is bullying others or your family would like to better communicate with one another to improve upon the quality and strength of the relationship between you and your children.

PART 1:
ORION AND BENNY

1

Have you ever had a moment that took your breath away? Not the good kind, but that kind that brings back a flood of memories you thought you had let go of and didn't care to remember?

I'm literally having one of those moments right now.

You will never believe who I just received a Facebook request from. Here I stand, at the kitchen counter, preparing my morning cup of coffee and checking up on Facebook before getting ready for my first class of the day and—bam!—now, I'm sitting.

There it is: the ultimate blast from the past. Well, not so much a blast, but it has been years since I last saw Benny.

Benny. To this day, I still cringe when I think of him. I would love to say this is a welcomed message, but, considering our past, I am hesitant to even click Accept.

Maybe I should start at the beginning for you to understand all of what happened between Benny and me. Better yet, I won't begin with the day it all started but from the day of my home invasion. When my only safe haven was ripped right out from under me by my mortal enemy, Benny. It's a period in my life when—no matter how hard I have tried—I can never forget and can't seem to totally let go of.

I remember it all so vividly, as if it just happened yesterday. The morning started off cold and gloomy, but that wasn't going to stop me and my dog, Rexy, from going on one of our epic adventures. The day before, we stumbled across a cool cave, and on the day in question, we were going back to investigate our new discovery.

Imagine the scene: We're both looking deep within the dark eerie cave, ready to explore, when out of nowhere, something flies out, skimming the top of my head. I quickly turn to see what it is, but it's already gone out of sight. I hesitate, afraid to take another step, but my brave sidekick, Rexy, takes his nose and nudges me further into the unknown. Where the uninviting comes crashing down on me, like a tidal wave, completely covering me in a gross, smelly, gooey slime.

As I wipe the slime from my face, my one eye squints open, revealing a ray of light casting a huge shadow upon the cave wall. Rexy and I slowly turn around to see a very large creature bounding right toward us. Without a second thought, we run further into the cave, hoping to escape but, instead, I end up entangling myself in a thick, sticky cobweb that's covering the cave walls. Frantically, I twist and turn, tangling myself even worse.

Rexy grabs onto the web in an attempt to free me, but it's everywhere and so sticky that it gets caught in his teeth. I pull with all my might until I am finally able to break free of the web. I run, stumbling over my own two feet, behind a boulder, pulling Rexy behind me by the web stuck in his teeth. As the creature leans in closer and closer, it opens its mouth wider and wider, revealing its huge very sharp teeth.

"This is the end! We're dinner!" I scream.

My voice is filled with fear as the creature roars, "Orion, it's time for dinner."

"Oh Mom, we were just getting to the good part," I say with great disappointment.

"You can play prehistoric times with Rexy another day.

Now, come out from under the dining room table, put your Batman sheets back on your bed, and clean up all this Silly String," Mom says. "Oh, and before we forget, take Rexy out for a walk, and fill his bowl with food in the laundry room. We have company coming for dinner and need everything spit-spot clean."

"Who's coming to dinner?" I ask with a bit of curiosity.

"Your father's new employee and his family. They have a son around your age. In fact, they are moving right down the street and are going to be our new neighbors."

"Great! I can't wait to meet them," I say, as she bolts around the house like Flash Gordon. Then I, too, start running around, pulling the sheets off the dining room table.

The doorbell rings, and I literally race out of my room, bound down the stairs, and come to a skidding halt as I slide into the backside of my mom.

"Well, you're not at all excited, are you?" She winks as she opens the door.

I can no longer take the suspense, and being so eager, I lose my mind for a moment. I unthinkingly nudge my mom out of the doorway to get a good look at my new friend when all of a sudden, I stop in my tracks and freeze.

"Orion, aren't you going to invite our guests in?" Mom smiles as she pats me on the back of my head, then leaves her hand there for a moment.

I just stand there, gazing, unable to move or say anything.

As Mom slides my frozen-stiff-as-a-board body to the side, she laughs and says, "Boys, where are their manners at times? Please, come in and make yourselves at home."

I'm stunned that it's Benny at my house…walking in my house, going to see my room, going to eat dinner at the same table as me—going to pummel me! Wait, he can't pummel me, because he's at my house with my parents. Even though Benny is the school bully, he can't do anything to me here, which gives me the teensiest glimmer of hope.

Let me just start off with, Benny's not your average bully; he's actually quite inventive with his bullying tactics, and in most opportunities, he has taken his bullying to an entirely different level.

First, he put water from the school's fish tank in my water bottle, where my first clue was the fluttering of fish fins in my mouth. Before I could even do anything, my teacher, Mrs. Zimny was calling my name out and sent me straight to the principal's office for trying to eat the class mascot.

Then, Benny took a picture of me where he Photoshopped a poufy hot-pink dress on me with a long blond wig and a humongous polka-dotted hair bow with the unforgettable caption, "Vote for our next prom queen, Orion." He posted the "prom queen" pictures all around school and online. Doesn't take a genius to guess who was the laughing stock of the school with the girls all posting beauty, makeup, and hairstyling tips on my locker door.

Once, he shoved me into a locker with smelly old socks, moldy red onions, and disgusting fish heads. I was literally trapped in the locker with no escape until Mr. Lewes heard me and let me out, where a putrid cloud of disgusting garbage-can stench surrounded me for the rest of the day.

Then there was the time Benny poured water on my chair right before I was about to sit down, and I had to walk around with a wet butt while everyone made jokes about me peeing my pants. To make it even more humiliating—because it's the gift that just keeps on giving—all during that week into the next, kids left diapers in my locker, in my backpack, and on bus seat—pretty much anywhere the other kids thought I might be.

Lastly, Benny looked pretty smitten with himself when he

came up with the "brilliant" idea to duct-tape me to the school flagpole with the sign Got Tape attached to my chest.

Tonight, after Benny's parents come inside my house, with Benny trailing behind, I shut the door. As he walks past, Benny turns to me, puts his right fist in my face, and shakes it with a smirk on his face. He then turns as if nothing was wrong and walks in the living room with his parents. I take a few steps backward till my backside hits the door, and I slide down the door until my bum hits the floor with a thud.

Really...Benny? I mean, really...Benny! I repeat in disbelief.

"Orion, Son, come in and join our guests," Dad calls from the living room.

I slowly come to my feet while every imaginable excuse flows through my head. "Coming," I yell out.

I take my time getting to the living room, dragging my feet along the floor. As I enter, I see Dad serving the Finklesteins drinks with them on the big couch and Benny sitting by himself taking up the entire loveseat like he owns the place, like he's "King Benny."

That's it! I whip around and yell out, "Coming, Mom," then scurry off to the kitchen, where she's preparing dinner. "Hey, Mom, I thought you could use some help in the kitchen. What can I do?" I say sweetly.

"Thank you for offering. Now, where is my son? What have you done with him?" She giggles.

"I'm right here. I just thought you might need some help. Umm, that smells good. What are we having?" Inquiring minds are looking for any excuse to escape this disastrous situation.

"If I didn't know better, I would think you were up to something," she says. "Well, if you really want to help, you can bring out that tray with the chips and salsa with Mrs. Finklestein's red wine."

Now, the whole point of me coming into the kitchen was to escape Benny, and now I'm being thrown back into the wolves' den. How did asking what's for dinner turn into me being King Benny's waiter?

Before I can even open my mouth, Mom hands me the tray with chips, salsa, and a very tall wobbly-looking glass of red wine and gently pushes me out the kitchen door into the living room (or should I say lions' pit?) where I picture Caesar giving his thumbs-down for Benny to pulverize me. As I back into the living room, I turn around and practically trip over Benny's protruding foot.

"Benny, pull your feet back so Orion doesn't trip," Mrs. Finklestein says sternly.

Whew, that was a close one!

I turn to see Benny glaring at me with his infamous smirk.

Did he purposely put his foot in my pathway with the intent of trying to trip me?

Luckily, Mrs. Finklestein has eyes in the back of her head. I'm pretty sure that airborne salsa and red wine are not a good thing. Unless, they were to land all over Benny. Now, that's funny.

If only... I giggle inside. *If only...*

2

After what feels like ten agonizing hours, I turn to look at the clock. Bam! Reality hits—fifteen minutes have passed. Only *fifteen* minutes...seriously? How can this be?

I stare at the clock over the fireplace.

If I can just mind-bend time, this horrific night could be over in seconds.

I focus on the clock that sits on our mantel that also happens to be where Dad keeps his pride and joy of a baseball collection that he can't resist showing off to the Finklesteins.

Worst of all, I'm stuck having to sit on the same loveseat with my "buddy" Benny because all the other seats have been taken.

While everyone admires Dad's cool baseball collection, Benny's busy flicking me in the back of my head, hard, anytime everyone's attention is pulled away in the opposite direction.

I want to scream at the top of my lungs, *Stop flicking me! Stop tormenting me! Stop beating up on me! Stop making me a laughing stock of the entire school! Stop...*

But I can't say anything, because who's going to believe me? Especially with Mr. Finklestein being Dad's new employee and friend. Until now, I was ecstatic and thankful that school had ended last week because I wouldn't have to deal with Benny's relentless bullying.

One of the worst incidents, one that ranks right up there with the infamous "Streaking Smurf" incident, would be the time we were playing Marco Polo in swim class. My eyes were closed with everyone around me in the water, and the next thing I know, my swimsuit is yanked down clear off me. I open my eyes to see my swimsuit flying through the air, in slow motion, making its landing on my secret crush, Jessica, with everyone laughing.

And the look on Jessica's face… Ugh, the humiliation.

Since that day, I've never been able to bring myself to speak to or look Jessica in the eyes, and she seems to avoid me every chance she gets. And that's just another example on the very long list of Benny's unrelenting bullying. And now, Benny, the biggest bully ever, is moving in the same neighborhood as me with our parents being new best friends.

My life is over as I know it. Next, my parents will be getting a divorce. My mom will marry Mr. Finklestein, and then Benny and I are stepbrothers. That's the only thing that could make this worse. My mind is racing, and I'm cringing at the thought of being Benny's stepbrother.

"Orion, did you not hear me?" Mom says firmly. "I have been calling for you to come help bring food to the table."

I'm so busy dreaming up a nightmare of me and Benny being stepbrothers that I lost track of hearing Mom. You know, they should have something called "daymares" instead of daydreams.

But my thoughts about these daymares don't last long as Benny snaps me out of it by giving me a good shove off the loveseat.

Mrs. Finklestein intervenes with, "Easy, Benny."

"Aw, Mom, I'm just helping my friend Orion here get a move on," Benny says with one of his mischievous grins.

I bring all the things Mom has lined up on the kitchen

counter to the dining room table in record time. Taking on a new strategy of thinking, I conclude, if I can warp-speed this night, it will be over in no time. I place the last dish on the table and scream out, "Dinner, come and get it!"

"Orion, really, must we scream?" She pokes her head in the dining room doorway.

"Just excited to eat this yummy food, Mom. You know me. I love a good dinner that satisfies my tummy right before bed." As if on cue, I muster up the most fake yawn to seal the deal.

She turns away to get something, so she misses the mimic of a yawn but catches the sound. "Wow, honey, you must really be tired. Is this what's gotten in to you?"

There it is—my out! She's giving me an out without even knowing it. I really have to try this more often. This is so cool. Wait, focus, just stay focused. As I regain the objective for the night, which is to warp-speed Benny out the door, I decide to let this play out.

"Oh yeah, Mom. Sorry, just so tired, had a long day with baseball practice and everything."

"Ok, we'll eat and see what we can do about wrapping up the night a little earlier than planned. It's all good. They're moving right down the street. So, we can do this anytime."

Anytime...*anytime*! The word just keeps repeating itself like an out-of-control race car going, at lightning-fast speed, around a never-ending circular speedway in my head.

Ok, hit the brakes and stay focused. First things first—get rid of Benny tonight, and tomorrow's another day, I try telling myself.

Dinner is all talking and laughing for the adults with Benny putting on his best show of getting along with me on the surface, but below the surface it's a different story. Under the table, he's putting his best foot forward in a masterful match of hide and kick with Benny kicking all over in the direction of me, trying to find and make contact with my dodging shins.

Benny's timing is impeccable. He has an unbelievable ability to strike and hit right when everyone's laughing. At one point, he excuses himself from the table to use the bathroom and returns about ten minutes later.

"Benny, you ok?" Mrs. Finklestein asks.

"Sure, Mom, just bathroom stuff," Benny replies, turning ten shades of red.

Oh yeah, one for Orion's team!

What I didn't know is that Benny, as usual, was up to no good.

Finally, it's dessert time, and I'm so eager to get rid of Benny that I'm about ready to jump out of my skin. My mom brings in the strawberry shortcake with fruit toppings to the table, including the sugar bowl, because who doesn't like fresh fruit topping with sugar over it?

Benny jumps up. "Mrs. Taylor, dinner was so good. I would like to show my appreciation by serving dessert to everyone and serving my new best friend, Orion, first." Now, if I didn't know better, I would think he was on the up and up.

Mom sits down, thanking Benny for being such a gentleman. "Maybe this will rub off on someone we know," she says.

Well, we all know who she's talking about as I look around and see big flashing red neon arrow pointing at me with a tiny version of Benny dressed as the devil, horns and all, with fire blazing from the top of his pitchfork while laughing in hysterics and jumping up and down on his left shoulder. Yes, we are all fooled by Benny, the devil in disguise. That is, everyone but me.

Benny continues his gentleman ways and asks me what I want every step of the way. "Sugar?"

"Of course, thanks!"

Benny pours on the sugar, and as he hands me my dessert, he "accidentally" (I mean, intentionally) knocks over the sugar bowl. "Oh, Mrs. Taylor, I'm so sorry."

"No harm, no foul. I'll just get us some more sugar. Be back in a flash." She dashes from the table to the kitchen and back with the sugar bowl refilled.

"Now, how about dishing me some of that delicious dessert, Benny," she says with a heartwarming grin.

"With pleasure, Mrs. Taylor," Benny replies with a smile.

Ok, who are we kidding?

I'm sitting here watching Benny, the master puppeteer, at work. Benny passes out the beautifully created dessert, and my suspicions grow.

"Dig in," Benny says.

Everyone at the table laughs and digs into Mom's well-known strawberry shortcake surprise. Talk about surprises. I dig in, put the spoon in my mouth, expecting a blast of fruit, cake, and sugary delight, when all of a sudden, my mouth puckers.

Benny must have put salt over my entire dessert. Is that what took him so long in the bathroom? He had gone to the bathroom all right, but did he make a pit stop in the kitchen to pour salt in the sugar bowl?

Everyone, and I mean everyone, at the table is gobbling Mom's delicious dessert. Well, almost everyone. I can barely open my mouth because it's so puckered in disgust. It's like the ocean has dried up in my mouth, and all that is left is a massive mound of salt.

"Orion, honey, are you ok?" Mom asks with concern. "This is your favorite dessert, and I made it especially for you."

I know I can't disappoint my parents on their special night of trying to impress the Finklesteins, so I willingly dive into one of the most disgusting things ever.

As I'm eating, I think back to "The Most Disgusting Thing" I was ever made to eat, thanks to my "good buddy" Benny. It had rained all night, so the next day at school, the grounds were covered with earthworms. Benny had come up with the bright idea of making a concoction he liked to call "chocolate with a wiggle" (consisting of earthworms, chocolate syrup, and dirt for added texture). Well, we all know how well that went down (or should we say, how well it made its return down to the ground from whence it came).

Ugh, that was totally gross. This is a piece of cake in comparison to that. In no time at all, I devour my dessert. No chewing involved. Just in the mouth and swallow.

"Mmmm. Mom, can I have more?" I blurt out eagerly, hoping a second helping of dessert will wash down and mask the nasty taste of the dried-up ocean in my mouth. That'll show Benny he is not going to get the best of me in my house.

3

The night is finally over with my mom, my dad, and me all at the door saying our good-byes. I stay behind, giving the door a real good shove and slamming it shut. *Don't let the door hit you in the...*

Mom comes back into the foyer. "Orion, can you be a bit more careful in not slamming doors...please." Then she says, "Wow, that was a great night! I think we are really going to be good friends, and you were great with Benny. He's such a well-behaved boy. I think the two of you are going to have a great summer together. Especially with them living right down the street." With a warm smile, she kisses me on the forehead and gently nudges me in the direction of the stairs to get ready for bed.

All that's going through my mind while getting ready for bed is the summer break I have been so looking forward to being "Benny-free," and now Benny is practically family. Every moment of bullying flashes through my mind, including the infamous Smurfing incident that gave me my humiliating nickname, "Streaking Smurf."

The moment plays out in my head as if it happened yesterday: Everyone was showering after gym, and I noticed the other kids watching me, but I couldn't figure out why. I had just poured my shampoo on my head and was lathering up like every other day after gym class. Next thing I knew, everyone was pointing and laughing at me, saying things like, "Look Papa, it's a Smurf" and so on. I was literally dumbfounded and had no idea what they were laughing at or talking about until…I looked down and saw my skin was blue.

It's a bit of a blur as to what happened next.

I quickly wrapped a towel around myself and ran out of the shower. Everyone, and I mean everyone, was laughing and pointing at me.

What was I going to do?

I was so shocked that I just kept running, right out of the locker room into the halls of the school.

It wasn't until the bell rang that I realized I was wearing nothing but a towel and feeling a huge draft. By then, to top it all off, kids were starting to file out of class.

I needed to escape!

So I turned back to the locker room and looked in the mirror. My face was literally purple, along with that lovely shade of blue. Then I ran into the shower stall and started rubbing my skin under the water with soap to wash the blue off. Only, it wasn't coming off. It actually took a few days for it to totally wear off.

In the meantime, Benny and everyone else were having a field day with the Smurf jokes, and like always, Benny got away with it because I had no proof, and no one was going to speak up against Benny for fear they would be his next target.

When I got home, my mom asked how I turned blue, and I was so ashamed, I just told her it was a lab experiment in science that went horribly wrong.

During the next few weeks, I made it my goal to keep from spending any time with Benny. I was successful until the Fourth of July. That's when the Finklesteins decided to have a barbecue to celebrate the holiday with just me and my parents, because by then they were besties.

The Fourth of July arrives, and I'm deep in thought.

What's the best way to tell Mom I'm sick, and I can't make the big night at the Finklesteins? Let's see, I could run really warm water over the thermometer, giving me a nice temperature. But I can't make the same mistake I did last time by running it under too hot of water and melting the tip off, casting beads of mercury everywhere. There would be no disputing a temperature, and we would have to stay home.

Oh man! Mom got rid of the old thermometer for the new and improved version of swiping it across your forehead. That's it! I, too, can be innovative in outsmarting a thermometer. I can take a really hot shower and right afterward have Mom take my temp. It has to work!

I waste no time. I jump in the hot shower and hop out after a minute or two. I then hightail it to my room where I leap onto my bed and pull the covers up over myself.

"Orion, get a move on, we're going to be late and you know how I don't like to be late," Mom yells up the stairs to me.

"Mom," I yell down. "Mom!"

"Orion, let's go!" she yells back.

"But, Mom, I need to see you. Can you come up for a minute?"

"All right, but it needs to be quick because we really can't be late." She reaches my bedroom and sees me in bed with the covers pulled up under my chin. "Orion, sweetie, are you ok?"

"Mom, I think I'm sick. I feel really warm," I say meekly as I pull out all the stops for the sympathy card.

"Ok, there's one way to find out. Let's take your temperature. I'll be right back." She heads to the bathroom to get the digital thermometer, quickly returns, and swipes my forehead. "Oh, thank heavens, you have a 98.9 temp. You're fine."

Now, I'm dumbfounded. I don't get it. That water couldn't have been any hotter. Why is my temperature not higher?

I sigh in bewilderment. "But, Mom, I really don't feel good. Look, here take my temp again, maybe the thermometer is broken."

"No, I know you, something's up. Now, tell me what's really going on."

I really can't say the truth because Mom thinks Benny is the sweetest boy. I feel the weight of hurting my mom with her new best friend and Dad's business heavy on me. I just can't bring myself to say anything.

"Nothing. I was just tired and wanted to stay home."

"Well, at least you didn't melt this thermometer like you did to the last one," she says with a wink.

I do a double take in disbelief. How did she know? Maybe she does have eyes in the back of her head. As she walks away, I look closely at the back of her head, examining it for any proof of the urban myth of moms possessing the superpower of eyes in the back of their heads.

With the Finklesteins living so close, we walk to their house, ready to share food and play games. The kind of fun that most kids would be excited about. My mind is instead filled with the thoughts of, *What's my good buddy Benny have in store for me tonight?*

My parents are so excited they miss seeing my startled reaction to the doorbell. My mom, who loves cooking, hands Mrs. Finklestein her fruit salad and famous blueberry pie, and my dad hands Mr. Finklestein a platter of ribs and steaks that he spent the afternoon making and applying his famous top-secret spice rub to.

Me, I'm more than dreading this evening, and that's putting it lightly. I just know I can't disappointment my parents and am somehow going to have to muster up courage and a smile for tonight.

Deep breaths. It's just one evening. I can do this.

As I lean in to peek from behind my mom, I see Benny, in the shadows, just lurking in the background like a cougar waiting for his moment to pounce. There is a single ray of light shining directly on Benny's glowing eyes, as if he has lasers beaming out of his eyes, penetrating my soul. In fear, I take a step backward while my mom gently nudges me through the doorway. I've just willingly stepped into what feels like Benny's fun house of horrors with the unknown awaiting to torture me at any moment. I stay close to my mom, using her as my human shield, in the hopes that Benny will leave me alone this time.

Mrs. Finklestein offers to give us a tour of their newly remodeled house, assuring us we will be ending the tour in the backyard, where everything is perfectly set up for the night ahead. While on the tour, I look around and notice everything in the house is in its place and lined up so perfectly and centered just right. Even Benny's room is the neatest room I've ever seen. It's kind of weird because you would never have known it was a child's room except for Mrs. Finklestein pointing it out.

"And, this is Benny's room. Excuse the mess. You know how boys can be."

Mess, what mess? Everything's perfect. Not one single thing is out of place, and you could skip a quarter (or better yet, bounce a person) clear across the room off Benny's bed. That's how tightly his blankets are wrapped. My mom would have heart failure if I kept my room like this. She would think I had been abducted and been replaced with a clone. (Note to self: get a clone that will make my bed like this.)

I scan Benny's room and notice all the plaques for honor roll and perfect attendance. Wow, I didn't think Benny had much going on up there. I just figured he was some dumb jock with a God complex that likes to amuse himself by making others around him miserable.

My mom points out how wonderful it must be to have a son on the honor roll each year.

Mrs. Finklestein jumps in without hesitation. "Well, not every year. See here, Benny couldn't get his act together and missed honor roll because of a B plus in art," she says, obviously disappointed.

Wow, my mom would be ecstatic bordering on hysteria—bouncing off of walls and jumping on furniture where we'd have to pull out the tranquilizer gun and dart her—if I were to make the honor roll. And, here Mrs. Finklestein is pointing out the one and only time Benny didn't make it. I'm a little taken back by this thought, as my eyes move from the plaques to looking around and wondering where are all the superheroes, Star Wars toys, electronic games, and so forth are stashed. Where are all the things that kids need to play with and be kids? I now begin to wonder if there are more reasons for Benny being a bully.

The tour ends, and everyone retreats to the backyard, where it turns out there are more people invited than just me and my parents. No other kids but more grownups to add to the mix. It also turns out Benny has a few cool things in the garage, one being water guns—the cool high-powered ones that can shoot across a backyard with precision. Then the unthinkable happens. For the first time ever, Benny and I play together like two boys who actually enjoy each other's company and have something in common.

Mrs. Finklestein lets Benny and me play with the water guns until it's time for dinner. By that time, both Benny and I are drenched from head to toe. "Orion, honey," she says warmly, "go with Benny and he'll give you some dry clothes to put on."

We both go off with Benny right on my heels. I'm about to enter his room when he forcefully grabs onto the back of my shirt, yanking me backward.

"Dude, what do you think you're doing?" Benny blurts out. "You can't go in my room with wet clothes! Boy, you must really be stupid! Here, I'll go get clothes for the both of us, and you can change in the bathroom."

Benny tosses a bunch of clothes at me, and I head to the bathroom to get changed.

About two seconds later, he's banging on the bathroom door. "Hey, loser, you done? What, you can't dress yourself without your mommy?"

I slowly open the door, praying Benny's going to keep his hands to himself. Instead, he pushes me to the side hard and rushes by me to get into the bathroom. As he gets dressed, I realize his shorts are way too big and I need a belt. Reluctantly, I yell through the bathroom door that I need a belt.

Benny, knowing his mom would get on him if I came downstairs with my shorts around my ankles, yells back, "Loser, go into the top drawer of my dresser on the left."

Here's where life becomes interesting and takes a turn into the unknown.

4

From inside the bathroom, Benny yells, "Top drawer."

But I left the bathroom door in a haste, missing the part about which drawer. I pull on the top right drawer of the dresser, and to my surprise, it's loaded with diapers.

Big kid diapers.

I'm mesmerized. I know I need to shut the drawer, but I'm unable to take my bulging eyes away from this glorious site. I've hit the jackpot!

All of a sudden, Benny comes in the room screaming at me to shut the drawer. He slams the drawer shut, nearly crushing my fingers in it. I turn to see Benny's face in the deepest darkest red-almost-purple I have ever seen anyone turn. "You tell anyone what you've seen, and you're dead meat!" he blurts out. "I'll pulverize you!" He then puts his fists right in my face, pressing them up against my nose and cheek while practically standing on my toes.

At that moment, I make a wise decision. I decide not to tell Benny he's in need of an entire box of breath mints and has a booger up his nose that keeps wiggling as he breathes, almost like its playing peekaboo. Instead, my natural instincts take over, and I cower down with a look of terror on my face.

Benny then puts his fists down and shoves me into the dresser. And without a word, he abruptly turns away and walks back down the stairs to the backyard, and I follow suit.

As I walk down the stairs in shock, I keep thinking, Benny the school bully wets the bed and wears diapers! Wouldn't that be the biggest headliner at school? Benny would be ruined, and he'd never be able to show his face without being humiliated. Yes, humiliated just the way he has humiliated me and all of the others like me for the past few years. I can't believe I finally have the ammunition I've been looking for to put Benny in his place. This explains where he got all the diapers to give to the kids when he played the wet pants prank on me.

Wow, I'm king of the world! Well, maybe not the world, but at least the school when all the kids hear about this. I'm a real-life hero! King Benny's rein is over, and I'm the one who's going to dethrone him and knock him on his butt. He won't know what hit him. He'll have to go into hiding. No wait, didn't he just say I was dead meat if I told anyone? Dead meat! That's dead meat like, I won't be around to live out my rein as King Orion. Can he do that?

It turns out to be the best night of my life. Benny, on the other hand, is as low key as I've ever seen him. He barely says a word at the dinner table. Yet, that doesn't stop him from shooting an eye-piercing glare at me every chance he gets. With desserts finished, Benny goes and whispers something into his mom's ear.

She, in turn, excuses him from the table, and he leaves the backyard to go into the house. She then turns to me. "I'm sorry, Orion. Benny's not feeling well and is going to turn in early."

"I hope Benny's feeling better soon," my mom chimes in. "We should be going too. Orion's had a long day, and he was pretty tired before coming over. We'll do this again real soon. We had a lovely time, and the food was delectable. We should do this at our house next time."

My mom gives Benny's mom a hug and kiss on the cheek before leaving. The walk home is quiet. My brain is in shock, and it is racing, trying to figure out my next move. The biggest move ever. The master of all moves that could change life as I know it. I just have to ruin and take down my mortal enemy to do it. This is a no brainer. Yet, I'm having difficulty in making a commitment to anything right now. Feeling confused, I shake it off. I pretty much have two months to make my life changing decision, and I decide to take the full two months.

You would think this would be one of the easiest decisions to make, but I've never had to humiliate someone to make myself feel better. Wouldn't this be considered defending myself and sticking up for myself and the defenseless others Benny has bullied? This is not a world I'm accustomed to. Can I be like Benny and humiliate and hurt someone to the core? The most important decision is, if I do it, would that make me any better than Benny? Wouldn't that make me a bully too?

As summer comes to a close, Benny's made himself pretty scarce since the infamous diaper incident. With his embarrassment keeping him hidden away, my summer vacation turned out to be pretty awesome and not as terrifying as I thought it would be thanks to my priceless discovery. All summer, I deliberate over what the right thing to do is. It includes some fun, comical skits of "What's It Worth?" A beat-up baseball with blown-out stitches—worthless. New baseball and glove—$85.00. Phillies game tickets—I don't know. Finding out Benny *Tinklestein* wears diapers—priceless!

Yes, Benny Tinklestein's new nickname is far more humiliating than Streaking Smurf.

Along with having some fun in the process, I also consider my options. Option number one: humiliate Benny in front of everyone at school by outing his deepest darkest secret. Option number two: tell my mom and/or my teachers about Benny's bullying in the hopes they believe me. Option number three: blackmail Benny. Last but not least (option number four): confront Benny about his bullying at the next dinner with the Finklesteins. Blackmail is pretty high up on the list and is tied with exposing Benny for who he really is and letting him suffer the consequences. Although, exposing Benny makes me consider the threat Benny made should I out his little secret.

There's also something else that's been weighing heavily on my mind the entire summer—what I witnessed at the Finklesteins' house during the tour. Especially when Mrs. Finklestein showed us Benny's room and chose to include the shaming of her son. Benny has so much pressure on him to be the perfect student and son. How can someone live up to such high expectations and not even get the acknowledgement for what they have accomplished? Only ever hearing about their failures and how they have to continuously do better and better. To work hard, do your best, and still not be good enough in your parents' eyes? My heart goes out to Benny for having to live under these conditions.

For me, it still doesn't justify or give Benny the right to take his frustrations and anger out on others. Making someone else feel bad and worthless just because his parents make him feel that way is no excuse. Even if nothing Benny does will ever live up to their high expectations, it is not right for him to take it out on those weaker than him. Maybe Benny's parents feel that they are realistic expectations, but for a child it can feel unobtainable. They are placing Benny under too much pressure, making it difficult for him or anyone to live up to their high standards of perfection. Still, Benny needs to learn he cannot bully people and get away with it without consequences, and he should be taught a lesson.

My struggle with deciding what is right is like a game of tug of war with my emotions and it consumes me until school starts again. At last, I have a revelation and make my final decision. I decide I'm not going to become a little mini Benny. Instead, I will take the high road of blackmailing, if you can call it that, in the attempt to teach Benny a lesson.

I don't want to have Benny's world crumble around him once his parents find out what he has been up to. On the other hand, I have not forgotten all the bullying that has been done to me and decide to only place the outing of Benny on the back burner in hopes my blackmailing keeps him in check and doesn't make him any angrier. My biggest concern is, I don't want Benny to make good on his threat of pulverizing me.

5

I'm ready in no time, in fact a half hour early, for the first day of school. As I get ready, I go over my mental check list multiple times. It's not only the first day of school, but a day that will go down in history as the day I stood up to the school bully and changed my life and others' as it was known forever. I'm going to be a hero. A silent hero but nonetheless a "hero."

"Orion, do you have everything you need for your first day?" Mom says as she reaches for my backpack.

As if on a springboard, I jump into the air and grab the backpack before Mom can reach it.

"Yes, Mom, I have everything I need. Remember, I'm a big boy," I say with a smile. Then I go over and give her a big hug. "I gotta go, or I'll miss the bus."

"Wow, you are a big boy, aren't you?"

"See ya later, Mom," I yell out as I shut the door and run down to the end of the driveway to wait for the bus.

The bus finally arrives, and I go to take my first step onto the bus.

One small step for man. One great leap for mankind.

I then sit down and wait patiently for Benny's stop. I sit there, gripping my backpack for dear life, with my knuckles turning white, for within the backpack is my weapon of choice that I'm going to use to defeat my mortal enemy, Benny.

My heart races, and everything starts to become jumbled in my mind as I try to go over the plan of attack. Each stop brings me closer and closer to the end with the threat of being pulverized looming over my fate. The bus is pretty full, and Benny's stop is coming up next. I take a deep breath and exhale slowing three times in an attempt to calm myself down and remain focused.

As Benny steps on the bus, everything and everyone around me freezes except for me and him. In slow motion, he steps closer and closer to me. This is it. The moment has arrived. Time no longer stands still, and Benny's practically standing right on top of me, but there are no seats available, so he gives the kid behind me one of his smirks and motions for him to get out of the way. The kid literally hurls himself out of the line of fire and takes a seat in the back of the bus. Benny flops down and bangs on the back of my seat, ensuring I know he has arrived.

"Hey loser! What's for lunch today?" Benny says as he reaches over and grabs my lunch bag. "Well, let's see what we have here." He takes the items out of the bag and unwraps each one.

Benny decides he needs to take a taste test to see if there's anything he would like to eat. Each time he bites into something, he yells out something gross and tosses the food over his shoulder to the back of the bus...except for my sandwich, which he intentionally drops on the bus floor, stating it needs some extra flavor, then smashes it with his boot. By the time Benny finishes, I have a bottle of water and a flat-as-a-pancake sandwich (that maybe Rexy would eat) left for my lunch.

The bus finally makes it to its final destination. Everyone starts to exit the bus and head to class with Benny pushing me back down in my seat as he bulldozes by me.

Well, that didn't go at all how I planned.

I need to take drastic measures. I take the photo of Benny's room I took on one of the times I was made to go to his house, and I tape it to the inside of his gym locker. The photo is of Benny's room with the infamous diaper drawer open. I then put a diaper in the locker, along with a note that I tape to the bottom of the photo.

Finklestein, I mean, Tinklestein. Yes, I said it—Tinklestein! You want your life to end as you know it then just try and bully me or any of my friends again and I will out you so fast your head will spin. Everyone, and I mean everyone, will know you wear diapers!

Gym class is over, and it's time to shower, change, and get to the next class. I make sure I finish showering faster than ever so I can be there for the unveiling. Benny, being his normal mean self, is cracking his towel on kids and making fun of them. Benny finishes toweling off and pulls the handle on his gym locker.

My entire body tenses up with my heart beating so fast I'm afraid it's going to beat right out of my chest.

It's the moment of truth. The moment I've been gearing up for all summer long. There's no turning back now, even if I wanted to. My stare is fixated on Benny and the gym locker that's going to change my life, everyone's lives, forever.

Benny lifts and pulls on the gym locker handle, opening the locker up all the way, giving it a bit of a bang with the door hitting on the locker next to it. Immediately, he shuts his locker with a slam and whips around to shoot a most evil eye-piercing glare directly at me.

Benny couldn't have had time to read the note, but sure

as anything, he saw the diaper and maybe even the picture. Now the question is, did anyone else? He looks as though he is seething, and if he could be foaming at the mouth like a rabid dog, he would be.

Benny takes his right fist and punches his locker, followed by opening it about a sliver of the way to get his dry clothes. He gets dressed as quickly as he can and storms out of the locker room, kicking the towel bin into the air with a bang, knocking towels everywhere.

I actually start to breathe again. I'm relieved because I thought I was going to be that towel bin.

For the rest of the day, I continue to look over my shoulder, just waiting for Benny to make good on his promise to pulverize me. To my surprise, nothing—and I mean, nothing—happens.

At the end of the day, everyone is getting on the bus to head home. Everyone except for Benny that is.

Where's Benny?

The bus ride home is uneventful but still stressful because maybe Benny's found a way home and is going to jump out and attack me at the bus stop. The bus pulls up to my stop, and I carefully look around in every direction to see if Benny is in sight.

No Benny. I don't get it. Could my plan have worked?

The next day, Benny's not on the bus on the way to school, but he is at school. Benny's roaming the halls, attending classes, and acting like any other normal average kid his age.

I feel as though I've stepped into the Twilight Zone, an

alternate universe, where Benny's been abducted by some other life form and been replaced with an alien.

There's a point where we pass one another in the hall, and Benny shoots me a glare but nods his head as if to say, *Touché, well played.*

I nod my head back in return as if to say, *Game! Match! Point! Score!* I have played the most masterful game of my life and come out victorious. I stepped into the arena, made a masterful move, and dethroned the undefeatable Benny Finklestein. Life is good!

6

"Orion, honey, time to get up for school," Mom anxiously yells up the stairs. "Come on, sleepyhead, you don't want to be late for your first day. Breakfast is ready and waiting."

Wait! First day of school? What? No way! How can this be?

In a state of bewilderment and shock, I shoot straight up out of bed like a rocket blasting off to an unknown world. Feeling something stuck to my cheek, I take my hand to peel off what seems to be a piece of paper glued to my face by my own drool. I look at the paper to see it's the infamous Benny Tinklestein locker note.

No! No! No! This isn't happening! I defeated Benny Tinklestein. It's over! It's over!

It's not over, I scream in my inside voice to myself.

Ugh, I dreamed it all, and now I have to start this day all over again. It's never going to be over.

I scramble around my room for my clothes and bound down the stairs to the kitchen, where Mom is serving breakfast to everyone. "Hey, it's about time you showed up," she says. "We were about to send Rexy up to revive you." She giggles.

I give a grunt, pull out my chair in a huff, and plop myself down in the chair. As I sit there slouched in my chair, barely acknowledging Mom and Dad while I stare into space and stew over what has happened, they become confused and concerned.

"Honey, what's wrong?" Mom pulls her chair closer to mine.

I look up and just stare at her with a blank look, not knowing what to say or where to even start if I were to say something.

"I have to go now, but I want you to call me at work later," Dad says to Mom. He then drinks the last drop of his coffee, grabs his briefcase, and heads toward the front door. On his way, he leans down to kiss me on my forehead, but I turn my head away in distraught manner.

"Son, I'm not sure what's wrong, but we need to sit down when I get home tonight," he says in a concerned tone. "Honey, have a good day, we'll talk later," he says to Mom as he closes the door behind him.

I'm left sitting at the kitchen table with Mom and Rexy, who's nudging me with his wet nose, trying to get the attention he looks forward to each morning from me. I'm dazed and unable to move a muscle. Feelings of helplessness rushing through my body and mind like a whirling tornado destroying everything in its path. I struggle, from deep within, to hold back a monsoon of tears just waiting for the flood gates to open.

"It's never going to end," I mumble to myself.

"What do you mean, it's never going to end? What's never going to end?" Mom asks.

It's at this moment that I realize I had not used my inside voice and actually said out loud what I was thinking.

"I just can't, Mom. You wouldn't understand."

"What won't I understand? You have me worried; please tell me what's going on. I can't help you if you don't tell me what's going on," she pleads with me.

In my mind, I'm weighing out my options. Which are come clean, tell Mom, and undoubtedly be pummeled by

Benny. Or don't tell Mom and live life as I have been for the past few years as a coward drowning in misery and continue to live with the looming cloud of doom of being pummeled by Benny and tormented on a daily basis. All I can picture is both options on a scale teetering and balancing out in my head. Pummeling carries a lot of weight behind it. Not much of a win-win. More like a lose-lose. I know I have to say something because I've already opened the can of worms.

This may have been a mistake but maybe a blessing in disguise. I've tried everything else in my arsenal with no relief or escape from Benny's relentless bullying. I ponder it for a moment or more. Finally, I open my mouth, but nothing comes out. Not a sound. I find myself holding my breath unable to breathe or utter a word. Fear has taken over my entire body and is holding it hostage.

Mom takes my hand in hers, and I see tears falling down her face as her worry for me takes over. She takes her other hand and covers my hand, holding my hand in hers. "I'm here... I'm always here. I love you with every fiber of my being. It hurts me to see you like this. Please, let me help you. Please, tell Mommy what's wrong." She looks me in the eyes with the same fear I have been dealing with for far too long.

I look down, then tilt my head downward. I'm embarrassed, humiliated, and too scared to tell her what Benny has been doing to me. Thoughts start racing through my mind. What if she thinks it's my fault? What if she thinks I just let him do these things to me? What if she thinks I'm a wimp? What if she can't really do anything and everything gets worse because I tell her? What if she doesn't believe me? What if...

My mom takes her hand and ever so gently places it under my chin. Then she lifts my chin till my eyes meet her eyes as if she read my mind. "Nothing you ever could tell me could make me think less of you or make me love you any less. Please, tell me. Do you want me to ask questions and you answer yes or no? Would that help you talk to me?"

After thinking for a moment or so, I nod my head up and down.

"Is it school?"

I nod yes.

"Did something happen in school?"

I nod yes.

"Did something bad happen in school?"

I nod yes.

"Does it have to do with your teacher?"

I shake my head side to side for no.

"Does it have to do with a grownup at school?"

I shake my head no.

"Does it have to do with how you are doing in school with a class?"

I shake my head no.

"Does it have to do with another child at school?

I hesitate for a moment but then nod my head slowly for yes.

"Is it more than one child at school?

I shake my head no.

"Does this child do mean things to you?"

I nod my head yes.

"Is it a boy doing these things to you?"

I nod yes.

"Does he ever touch you to hurt you?"

I put my head down and nod yes.

"Does Mommy know this boy?"

I nod yes, and while nodding I leap into her lap and arms, sobbing.

"Is it Benny?"

I literally can't speak because I'm crying so hard but nod my head yes while pulling back from her to look at her. "How did you know?" I manage to squeak out.

"I didn't know, but when I think back to this summer and all the things you normally love to do but didn't do when it came to spending time with the Finklesteins, it all makes sense now. Honey, why didn't you come to Mommy and Daddy? You have to know that we would never allow anyone to treat you badly or hurt you no matter who they are."

"But it's Dad's employee, and you guys are best friends. I didn't want to cause any problems," I say through my sobs.

"You could never cause a problem! If you need us, we are here for you, no matter what. Well then, it's going to make it all the easier to talk with Benny's parents," she says will a warm smile.

All of a sudden, I'm flooded with an overwhelming urge rushing through my body, like the waters surging through a damn breaking away, and I begin to tell my mom everything about Benny and all his relentless bullying.

"Sweetie, I'm so, so sorry. I am sorry that I missed this, sorry that I didn't see it happening. I love you, and I would never let anyone hurt or harm you in any way. I'm so glad you finally opened up and told me. I know how hard this is for you, and you have never been a bigger boy then you are right at this moment. We will make this right....I promise. I'm so very proud of you."

I look up into her teary eyes and sputter out, "Proud of me...why?"

"Why? Because it takes a courageous and strong person to look his or her fears in the eye and meet it head on and talk about it."

At that moment, I latch back onto her for dear life and hug her so tightly she can barely breathe. "I love you, Mom!"

My first day of school that year became a life lesson I will never forget. Hiding the truth about what was happening didn't help me. It kept me from sharing my life with my family. Being honest with my family saved me that day. Once Benny's parents learned what was happening to me, things changed. For the better. The truth set me free.

Oh, the joy of life and being able to be kid again. Life was good!

As far as what happened to Benny, Mom and Dad had a heart-to-heart with Benny's parents, who were, needless to say, pretty upset. Mr. and Mrs. Finklestein weren't as receptive to my parents' intervention as they thought they would be. Mr. Finklestein gave his two-week notice to my dad, and within a month or so, they had moved to another town or even state. We never knew where they went, and for what seemed like forever, I never heard from Benny.

My only hope, in all these years, was that Benny would receive the love and support from his parents or a teacher or someone who could get him the help he so desperately needed.

And I hoped the truth would set him free like it did for me.

7

So, as you can see, I'm conflicted about Benny's friend request. My curiosity has gotten the best of me, but who wouldn't be curious in this situation. I feel this compelling need to accept Benny's message request—if for nothing else, just for some closure for myself.

I'm literally sweating, and my heart is racing, as though it could beat right out of my chest. How does he still have this effect on me? I'm a grown man, and still this person puts a jolt throughout my body. Everything is resurfacing and emerging out of the depths of my suppressed emotions. Emotions that only Benny has ever been able to pull the trigger on.

I've been so guarded with my emotions and in being able to trust others. Everyone sees this confident individual who has it all together because that's what I portray and want them to see. I'm never going to let anyone do to me the horrible things Benny inflicted upon me physically or mentally.

But no matter how much I try to convince myself, the reality is, the impact Benny had on me has never really left me. Time and again, I have tried to convince myself that it had left me, but it's always there lurking in the background, like an unshakeable shadow. From that momentous morning with my mother, in the kitchen, I have been fearless as far as facing my fears. Internally, I can't seem to let anyone in. I mean, really in. It's not fear so much as a defense mechanism. I'm not a victim per se, yet I feel like a victim to my own emotions. All I know is I have worked so very hard to get to where I'm at now, and I'm going to continue to work on where I'm going emotionally. And, I think accepting Benny's request could play a big part in the process.

What are my options? It's a 50/50 outcome: Either he apologizes, or he tries to cyberbully me and I click "Delete." Either way, it's part of my healing process. I thought I had moved on, but clearly, subconsciously I have not. This is Benny's and my final chapter. If I'm going to do this, it's now or never.

I'm clicking Accept. Done!

> *Hey, it's Benny... I would really like to catch up with you.*

No turning back now.

> *I wasn't so sure you would accept my request considering everything that happened between us, but I am glad you did. So much has happened, and I've changed a great deal from the young boy you once knew.*
>
> *I know, it was kind of weird how me and my family pretty much disappeared after your parents confronted mine. We literally stayed in contact with no one. And my parents, well, they just tried to make everything fade away into the background like nothing ever happened. At least, in the public's eye, but behind closed doors it was a different story.*
>
> *After your parents had a sit-down with my parents, my old man went totally ballistic. I'd never seen him so mad. Other than school, I was on house arrest, and any spare time I had was taken up with studying or chores around the house. After the move, my parents made a decision to place me in military school.*
>
> *But, it just didn't seem like anything helped. It was like*

falling down a rabbit hole but with no means to get out. Just darkness with no light in sight. So, I continued to spiral downward and rebel to the point my grades were all slipping. I was on the verge of being expelled. Now, that caught my parents' attention 'cause grades were everything to them, and perfection was the be all to be all. But, I'm sure, if anything you remember that.

I was then placed in what they call a boot camp for problematic kids. It wasn't so much the camp but Captain Walker who turned my life around. He did what no one else had done. Took an interest in me and my individual potential, showed me I was worth something, and didn't give up on me. I needed to not only learn to respect my parents but respect myself and to live my life for me and not my parents. I needed to learn that I am worth loving and that love starts with loving one's self.

Trying so hard to prove myself to my parents that I was good enough on every level and I deserved to be loved was something I didn't know how to deal with. It was a never-ending losing battle. I was in a dark desperate place where I lashed out and tried to do anything and everything to try to fill the void and take my pain, frustrations, and resentment away.

But, nothing ever seemed to work. Even my body rebelled against me. I'm still ashamed to admit that I wet the bed till I was in my teens. After Captain Walker straightened me out and placed me on the track to healing emotionally, my bed-wetting miraculously stopped. Emotionally, I was now equipped to start leading a normal life in all aspects. Well, as normal as one can be expected. No one's life is perfect, but I'm never reverting back to the horrid person I once was.

Believe it or not, I always thought you were a cool kid. That being said, I have to say, I was really jealous of you and the relationship you had with others. And then when I saw you with your parents, that just sealed it. I'm still pretty distant from my parents. See them on holidays and that's about it. We never connected like you and your parents and our relationship was always strained by their never-ending need for perfection and excellence. I've come to grips with not being able to live up to my parents' high expectations of me. And, now, I'm happy living for me and just being me.

I know nothing I have said excuses, in any way, the horrible things I inflicted upon you. I deeply regret and am more than ashamed of my past actions. If I could take it all back, I would but sadly, that's not possible. I can only hope that you accept my sincerest apologies. And, I hope can somehow find it in your heart to forgive me.

Heart racing, I think about the life that Benny was forced to lead. How he used all his fear and anger on me to try to feel worthy. I couldn't imagine how lonely it must have been for him. I wish now I had known a way to reach out to him as a kid. To that kid I spent time with on the Fourth of July one summer night. I wrote back:

I admit, I didn't want to click accept. Some part of me had buried the pain and shame I had at letting myself be treated that way. I am surprised and relieved by your message. I appreciate, more than you know, you reaching out to me and apologizing for all that we went through. I can feel your sincerity and remorse. I never thought, in a million years, this would happen, but I accept your apology and wish I could have been your friend when we were kids, instead of your target.

I'm so glad your life has turned around in a positive

manner. I've thought about you through the years and had hoped someone had reached you and helped guide you to your inner strength in healing you emotionally into becoming a better person. I really hope you are finding acceptance and happiness now. We have a chance now to make life better for ourselves.

I typed those words with full honesty. No more secrets, no more keeping things buried. Just the freedom of two people finding peace.

Benny messages back:

Right! Thank you for accepting my apology. I really wasn't sure if you would. I would have totally respected and understood if you had not. You accepting my apology means a great deal to me. For you were impacted the most by my horrid actions and took the brunt of it all. I have a few more people to contact, but I wanted you to be the first. Maybe we can get together sometime for a drink and talk more?

I can see the hope in his words to reconnect and find common peaceful ground. For the first time in years, I am excited about this new friend.

I would like that. I have to run off to class. Catch ya later! I type back.

Later it is!

8

I lean back in my chair, my coffee cold, and I realize that life itself is profound and humbling. How we treat others, at any age, has a great effect on them and those around them in all aspects of their life.

It means the world to me to receive this message from Benny, and I can tell what you must be thinking. No, his apology didn't take away the painful memories and the abuse he inflicted upon me. But it did give me closure and hope. That was a traumatic chapter in my life, and the ability to accept his heartfelt apology opened up my eyes to what I had been burying for years.

It allows me to continue to heal from within and maybe not forget but be able to forgive Benny for his abusive actions. That forgiveness isn't just for Benny—it's for me. It is a healing for my life. Holding onto pain and anger is unhealthy and can alter how we view life and others in how we interact in any type of environment and relationship.

Life is still good and even better now that Benny has become the man he was meant to be. It's never too late to take ownership of one's actions and initiate the healing process for all involved. I believe that anyone can change their stars, and one should never stop believing. Most importantly, once fear takes hold of you, it will stifle you. So face fear head on and conquer it, as I did. I will continue to do so, and so can you. Speak up and let the truth set you free.

PART II:
VICTIM OR BULLY?

1

WHAT IS BULLYING?

This chapter is intended to bring to light helpful information about bullying and how to identify if your child is a victim or a bully. It's also to help assist parents in opening the lines of communication among children and their parents and help parents gain a better understanding of what their children need from them to be more effective parents.

This is a brief discovery stage and not an in-depth knowledge-based book. For further assistance, beyond the pages of this book, please seek the assistance of a trained professional if your child is being bullied or is a bully, or your family would like to better communicate with one another to improve upon the quality and strength of the relationship between you and your children.

Bullies do not discriminate. Anyone—no matter your religion, race, color of skin, disabilities, age, gender, size and shape, beliefs, status in society, or relationship—can be targeted for bullying or be a bully. No one is off limits when it comes to a bully seeking out his victim, and no one is beyond bullying other human beings. It's a choice to bully another human being. No matter the reason, bullying is wrong on all levels and needs to stop!

A bully does not possess a distinctive face, meaning, a bully could surface anywhere at any time and be anyone from a stranger, school mate, friend, or even a family member. It's more disheartening and devastating when it's a friend or loved one inflicting the pain—someone you have put your love, faith, and trust in. It's very disturbing when a child is being victimized by another child or worse, the unthinkable, a family member.

Opening the lines of communication is essential in any healthy relationship. Especially with your children. There are two sections of questions to help aid you in opening the lines of communication with your child. Chapter 2's questions are for you to ask your child. Chapter 3's questions are for you to ask of yourself as the parent. You may also phrase some of the questions for the parent to the child to gain a better understanding of how your child perceives your relationship in helping your child's needs being acknowledged and met.

The questions are to assist you in your relationship with your child and help you gain a better understanding of your child and his or her life and needs, as well as how your actions and interactions, verbal and nonverbal, may be indirectly and/or directly affecting his or her life and behavior—whether it be positive or negative. The questions are to be thought provoking and a means to opening up communication between you and your child. They are to assist you in bringing to light if your child is a victim of being bullied.

The questions are not intended to solve and/or be the answers to a situation. If you find your child is being bullied, you need to take appropriate lawful measures in helping your child. If you find your child is bullying other children, then you need to take appropriate lawful measures, which may or may not include counseling.

Children learn their actions from somewhere and someone. Children, like adults, can adapt to their environment, and if the environment is too difficult for them to handle, then they develop a coping mechanism. For each child, that coping mechanism can differ, and for some, bullying in some way, shape, or form provides the means to being able to deal with a difficult situation in their inescapable environment.

A child's environment can directly affect their interactions with others, how they treat their peers, and how they view the world and themselves. Some children feel powerless and use bullying as a means of being able to control something or someone in their life. Other children feel bad attention is better than no attention at all and will do anything they can to get that attention. And some children rebel through whatever means they can to reflect the disapproval and unhappiness they are experiencing. Some children are "monkey see, monkey do" and will exhibit the positive and negative qualities they experience firsthand. Some children are looking for an outlet for their pent-up anger and frustrations and find bulling others allows them a means to unleash and release. There are some children who create an alter ego to take on and handle what's too difficult for them to deal with in their own reality. Still others feel worthlessness and have low self-esteem about themselves, and they intentionally seek out and find avenues to degrade and put down others in the attempt to build themselves up and feel good about themselves.

A child may know no different because through their living environment, they have been shown what is expected to be normal and acceptable behavior or have developed coping mechanisms to deal with the reality they are so desperately trying to escape. We are all a product of our environment.

Children do not possess the power to alter their environment and/or life's tools they have been given to work with. The divine truth can be unearthing and disturbing, but it is essential for a child's well-being. Change is essential and inevitable for all involved should your child be a bully.

You can place two children in the same unhealthy living environment yet have two distinctive separate results as far as adverse effects and the level of severity of those effects that the environment produced or exasperated. Either way, each child will be affected negatively, but it's how the child manages the environment and what coping mechanisms are created to deal with their environment that differs. What may seem like a well-adjusted, stable, and unaffected child can be deceiving on the outside, for within they are full of chaos and uncertainty in how they perceive life, themselves, others, and relationships.

Just because they do not act out does not mean they have not been affected by their environment. It also doesn't mean, in the future, their internal turmoil will remain internalized. Children develop coping mechanisms, which range from an emerging bully being released into the world to the total opposite of the spectrum where the child conjures up an inner strength from deep within that they cling onto for dear life because their survival depends on it.

There are still negative effects on the child who internalizes and/or focuses on their inner strength to get through the turmoil in their life. These children have tendencies to find something within their life that they can control since their environment is spinning out of control. It may show up in their grades, weight control, appearance, interests, extracurricular activities, etc. as far as being a perfectionist, and at times they take it to the extreme. This, in and of itself, is unhealthy. This is separate from being the best you can be by challenging yourself and pushing yourself to be and do better. It becomes overly consuming and can take over their life, creating other issues and concerns. They tend to feel they are never good enough for anyone and have difficulty in finding and maintaining healthy relationships.

The results can fill an entire book, for there are numerous consequences to an unhealthy living environment and the adverse effects on a child. This was just to give you an idea that what you see on the outside may not be what's happening on the inside.

The following are some behavioral changes that may be a warning sign that your child is being victimized by a bully, bullying others, or something in their life has taken ahold of them in such a way that they're acting out of character. Either way, as a parent, it is essential that the lines of communication be opened up to finding the underlining catalyst affecting their out of character actions and take the necessary steps in resolving the issue at hand.

- Dressing differently to the extreme
- Eating significantly more or less
- Significant weight gain or loss
- Personal hygiene being neglected
- Cranky, upset, crying, emotional, or easily agitated
- Having trouble sleeping
- Significant change to their appearance
- Loss of interest in any activities or something they normally enjoy doing
- Avoiding a person or a situation
- Avoiding answering questions about school other than academics, very short or curt in their answers, and/or seem agitated and/or uncomfortable and/or apprehen-

sive in answering any questions
- Coming home and going straight to their room
- More bumps and bruises than normal
- Avoid answering where or how they got hurt or a bruise
- Grades slipping or have plummeted
- Difficulty in concentrating
- Fatigued
- Falling asleep in class
- Acting out or being defiant at home or school
- Distancing themselves from friends and/or family members

Most children like to assert their independence by trying to handle things that are happening on their own. They don't want to be seen as weak or unable handle or deal with events in their life. Children tend to openly and willingly share the good things that happen in their everyday life but at times are reluctant to share anything negative that occurred. There are numerous reasons as to why children are not as open when it comes to voicing anything other than the positive aspects of their life.

First, children are more careful in filtering what they divulge because they don't want to change their parents' perception of them in a negative way. Some don't want their parents to see them as weak or vulnerable. Others are too humiliated and ashamed to even utter the words. Some children are under a threatening influence of being harmed if they tell anyone and that fear silences them. Others feel it would be tattling and don't want the stigma of tattletale following them around like an unshakable shadow. Some children feel that their parents wouldn't understand and/or expect them to deal with it on their own. Finally, some are in fear of their parents or a person of authority not believing them while others fear the repercussions of speaking up and what that means all around for them and the bully. They want to be seen as a big boy or girl and feel if they show they can't handle working out a disagreement on their own that they will be perceived differently in their parents' eyes and may have responsibility and/or privileges removed as a result and be treated differently.

2

QUESTIONS FOR PARENTS TO ASK THEIR CHILDREN

The following are questions for you, as a parent, to ask of your children. How you phrase the questions appropriately will depend on the child's age and comprehension level.

- Do you like school? What don't you like about going to school?

- Do you have anyone you stay away from? Why?

- Does anyone pick on you or call you names? What do they do? What names do they call you?

- Does anyone ever hit, slap, pinch, punch, push, kick, trip, pull your hair, or touch you in any way that makes you feel uncomfortable? What do they do to you?

- Does anyone ever spit on you?

- Does anyone ever throw anything at you or on you? What do they throw at you or on you?

- Does anyone ever trap you in something? What do they trap you in?

- Does anyone ever stand in your way and not let you by?

- Does anyone ever physically hold you down or against something or forcefully hold you preventing you from leaving a situation?

- Does anyone ever exclude you from anything? What are they excluding you from? How are they excluding you?

- Does anyone pick on you and make fun of your skin color? What do they say?

- Does anyone pick on you and make fun of your religion? What do they say?

- Does anyone pick on you and make fun of your height or weight? What do they say?

- Does anyone pick on you and make fun of your disability? What do they say?

- Does anyone ever do anything mean to you or treat you badly? What do they do to you?

- Does anyone ever make you feel bad? How do they make you feel bad?

- Does anyone write mean things about you? What do they write?

- Does anyone post anything about you anywhere that's mean? What do they post and where?

- Does anyone ever touch your belongings when you don't want them to or damage anything of yours? What do they touch and/or damage?

- Does anyone ever touch you in ways you don't like? How do they touch you? Where do they touch you?

- Does anyone ever make you eat anything you don't want to eat? What do they make you eat?

- Does anyone ever make you be mean to someone else? What do they make you do? What do they use against you to make you do something you didn't want to do?

- Does anyone make you feel afraid of them? What do they do to make you feel afraid of them?

- Does anyone threaten you? What do they threaten you with?

- Does anyone do any of these things to someone else in school, or are you they only one? Who? And what do they do to them?

- How does it make you feel when someone _____?

- Have you told anyone, and if so, who have you told? What happened after you told?

- If this is happening to others, have they told anyone, and what happened when they told?

- Do you know why he or she is doing these things to you?

3

QUESTIONS FOR PARENTS TO ASK THEMSELVES

The following are questions for you, as a parent, to ask yourself. You may also phrase some of the questions for the parent to the child to gain a better understanding of how your child perceives your relationship in helping your child's needs being acknowledged and met.

The only way this is going to work is if you're completely honest with yourself and in your answers. It's difficult anytime we put a mirror up to ourselves and look deep within right down to the inner core of our existence. This exercise is not only for the health and well-being of your child but also for yourself and any other family member in the household. Not only can you pose these questions to yourself and your relationship with your child, but many are also key questions to aid and assist in an adult relationship with your significant other (when appropriate, insert husband or wife or partner in a question).

Your next step depends on your answers to the questions. If there are any red flags or concerns, there may be a need to take immediate action, in a heathy direction for all involved, in seeking out the aid of a trained professional.

- Do I praise and/or acknowledge my child for a job well done?
- Do I stop and take notice of what's happening in front of me, or am I too busy to take a moment to do so?
- Do I spend enough quality time with my child?
- Do I tell and show my child I love him or her enough?
- Does my child know I love him or her no matter what?
- Do I take time to really get to know my child?
- Do I take the time to let my child get to know me?
- Do I ask my child how his or her day went and what he or she did?
- Am I too strict?
- Am I not strict enough?
- Am I too hard on my child?
- Do I set too high of expectations?
- Are the expectations I set obtainable and realistic for my child's capabilities?
- Do I set boundaries and limits for my child?
- Am I a good role model for my child?
- Am I trying to live my life through my child?
- Am I letting my child be himself or herself, or am I limiting my child's growth and potential?

- Does my child have a heathy balance of education and playtime/down time?

- Do I encourage my child that he or she can be whoever they want to be when they grow up?

- Do I encourage my child that he or she can do anything they set their mind to and they should at least try before giving up?

- Do I encourage my child to hope and dream and believe in himself or herself and his or her capabilities?

- Do I encourage my child's creativity and imagination?

- Do I let my child know I believe in them and always will?

- Do I make my child feel that what he or she does is good enough, or is pretty much everything my child does not good enough in my eyes?

- Am I always finding fault in everything my child does?

- Do I compare my child with someone else in front of my child?

- Is my child confident?

- Does my child look people in the eyes?

- Does my child avoid eye contact with certain people?

- Does my child flinch when people come near him or her?

- Does my child flinch when a certain person comes near him or her?

- Does my child exhibit any signs of being uncomfortable around a particular individual?

- Does my child come home hurt or with unexplainable marks and/or bruising on his or her body (where he or she avoids trying to answer what happened)?

- Have my child's grades plummeted or declined from their

obtainable potential?

- Does my child come home from school and go directly to his or her room, avoiding interaction with others (where normally they interact and then maybe take some alone time for homework and/or down time)?

- Is my child nice and kind?

- Is my child a quitter?

- Is my child showing his or her emotions or bottling them up?

- Is my child more emotional than normal?

- Does my child have a positive or negative attitude on life in conversations or activities?

- Is my child acting excessively positive and enthusiastic (as if overly compensating for something)?

- Is my child gaining or losing weight when he or she is at a healthy weight?

- Is my child dressing differently to an extreme?

- Is my child's hygiene declining, or does he or she no longer care about personal hygiene?

- Is my child fatigued, having trouble sleeping at night, and/or sleeping a good part of the day away?

- Is my child out of control at times?

- Is my child defiant, a trouble maker, or aggressive?

- Does my child have many friends, or does he or she stay secluded?

- Does my child have to always control a situation with me or others?

- Does my child put an emphasis on being a perfectionist? If I praise my child for something, does he or she only point out what could have been done better and not acknowledge praise or the positive?

- How does my child interact with peers? Do they seem to be on common ground, or is my child controlling what his or her peers say and do? Does it seem like my child is on the outside looking in?

- Does my child have anger issues and/or behavioral problems?

- Am I afraid of my child?

- Has my child ever threatened me?

- Has my child ever laid a hand on me in anger?

- Has my child ever tried to harm himself or herself?

- Is my child covering areas or parts of his or her body that he or she wouldn't normally cover or hide?

- Do I know where and who my child is with at all times when he or she is not with me?

- Do I give my child a way of getting ahold of me when he or she is not with me?

- Does my child feel he or she can come talk to me (and if not why)?

- Do I have good communication with my child?

- Do I trust my child?

- Do I feel my child is honest with me?

- Do I tell others nice things about my child, or do I mostly say negative things about my child and complain?

- Do I mostly yell at my child or talk to my child?

- Do I anger easily?

- Do I swear in front of my child?

- Do I lose my patience easily?

- Do I ever throw anything at my child?

- Do I ever try to hurt or harm myself in the presence of my child?

- Do I ever throw, punch, or kick things when I get upset?

- Do I push my child?

- Do I grab my child hard on any part of my child's body?

- Do I lose control and break objects in the home?

- Do I threaten to break something because I'm so upset?

- Do I ever lay an abusive hand on my child?

- Do I ever put my child in the middle of an argument with my significant other?

- Do me and my significant other argue in front of my child?

- Has my child ever seen me or my significant other ever lay an abusive hand on the other?

- Has my child ever witnessed me or my significant other emotionally abusing the other?

- Do I ever make my child choose between parents?

- Do I degrade the other parent in front of my child?

- Do I respond positively when my child is playing a sport, involved in an activity, being creative, or pursuing a hobby? Or do I always find fault and have something to say negative about what they have done and/or how they can do better next time?

- Do I set the example with being polite and respectful of others?

- Am I accepting of people who have differences like race,

religion, disabilities, physical appearance, and weight?

- Do I normally put a negative spin on things, or am I optimistic?

- Do I lead by example with showing my child the importance of family and friends?

- Do I instill in my child how important it is to share so everyone gets to take a turn who wants one?

- Do I instill in my child the importance of allowing everyone to have an opinion and to let everyone have a voice and be heard?

- Does my child spend more time in front of the TV or playing video games than talking with me or doing something together or doing something constructive and active?

- Do I ensure that the TV programs, movies, and games my child is exposed to are age appropriate, and do I eliminate anything with violence?

- Do I monitor my child's computer/phone time, ensuring they are not on sites that could be inappropriate and/or harmful or interacting with possible predators or someone who could harm them?

- Do I engage my children in conversation and activities?

- Do I set aside quality time for just me and my children?

- Do I mute my child or others by putting words in their mouth and/or speaking over them, not giving them a chance to voice their views, feelings, and thoughts?

- Am I a hands-on parent, or do I mostly let others take care of my children?

- Do I find myself putting things off with my child so much that my child no longer asks to do things with me or talks to me about things in his or her life?

- Does my love come with conditions?

- Do I degrade my child in any way and make him or her feel ashamed to be himself or herself?

- If my child is overweight, am I supportive and understanding in their struggle? And there to help and encourage them to eat healthy and exercise? Or, do I make my child feel ashamed and put undue stress and pressure on them to be a certain weight no matter the price?

- Have I been understanding, supportive, and loving with my child when he or she exhibited signs of being gender confused or came to me telling me he or she is a different gender on the inside and/or wishes to change their gender?

- Have I been understanding, supportive, and loving with my child when he or she came to me telling me he or she was attracted to the same gender?

4

WHO ARE BULLIES?

A Bully is…
> **B**eing controlling
>
> **U**gly behavior
>
> **L**ooking to victimize
>
> **L**onely existence
>
> **Y**earning for acceptance

Bullies crave attention, validation, and acceptance, and if they do not receive these affirmations on their terms, then they forcefully take what they so desperately need and desire.

A bully can emerge at a very young age where he or she can be as young as a four-year-old child right on up through adulthood and into one's elderly years. A bully may not fully emerge until they are of a mature age, showing that the transformation can happen anytime to anyone inclined to exhibit abusive behavior either due to their environment and/or coping mechanisms.

CHARACTERISTICS OF BULLYING

Bullying is a form of emotional and/or physical abuse that can be defined by the following characteristics:

Power Imbalance. A bully selects his or her victim by targeting someone they perceive as vulnerable. It's a natural selection process for a bully. A bully cannot bully an individual who is not susceptible to their power and influences. Instilling fear is a bullies most prominent primitive weapon.

Deliberate. The entire purpose of a bully's existence is to find victims to intentionally hurt in any way they can through emotions and/or physically. A bully has no boundaries, and anything and everything is fair game for them to utilize however they please when trying to inflict emotional and/or physical pain upon their victims. It's never by accident that a bully bullies someone. There are no apologies given or remorse shown—only relentless attempts to unleash what they are feeling from within on someone else to escape their environment or mask unresolved emotions to past experiences or treat others as they have been shown is acceptable behavior.

Repeated. A bully frequently targets the same victim over and over and over. Why? Because he or she can. It's far easier then seeking out another victim when in the bully's mind there is an existing victim all primed and prepped, waiting to be bullied. What draws a bully in further is someone who is ashamed or afraid to tell anyone about the abuse they are being subjected to, therefore ensuring the bully has a victim for the period of time they delegate to that victim before moving on to their next victim.

TYPES OF BULLYING

Bullying shows up in many different forms with the level of severity ranging from slight to off the charts. Here are some examples of many:

Physical. Tripping, hitting, punching, pinching, beating up, pushing, poking, throwing something at someone, spitting on someone, pulling hair, kicking, touching in any way that is not welcomed by the other person, locking someone in something, destroying or defacing personal property, holding someone so they are unable to move or get away and escape from a situation, grabbing someone very hard where it hurts.

Verbal. Threatening to harm, yelling, screaming, teasing, name calling, insulting, character bashing, mocking, using fear to control you, threats to harm someone else if you do not comply.

Relational. Excluding, spreading rumors, posting humiliation pictures anywhere (on posters, via texting, online), telling lies, involving others to hurt someone, ignoring, shaming, holding information over someone to control them.

APPROACHES USED BY BULLIES

Just as there are different types, methods, and levels of bullying, there are also different approaches bullies use when they bully their victim. The most commonly utilized, at school age, are the closet bully and the power over the masses approach.

The closet bully. Some bullies may only exhibit their bullying tendencies in front of their victim and no one else. It's an ugly secret where the skeleton is shoved in a dark cramped closet, hidden from the world under lock and key with the bully pocketing the key for his own personal use. You could be in public or in the presences of another person and the bully acts as though you're the best of friends and exhibits not one bullying characteristics toward you.

Power over the masses. For some bullies, it's all about holding the power over the masses, like in a school setting. The bully may only target one or two individuals but does it outwardly in public for all to see to be fearful of. All should be afraid and abide by the bully's rules, because those who do not live in fear of being made an example of become the bully's next target for abuse. This is not the trait of a leader but an out-of-control dictator who uses abusive means to rule over and control his subjects for his own personal gain.

Bullies intentionally bait, antagonize, and push as many hot buttons as they can in the attempt to find your emotional triggers. They then use those triggers, slowly chipping away at you till they reach your inner core. Once they reach your core, a bully then focuses on using anything and everything against you, within their arsenal of tactics, to control, manipulate, and hurt you.

Bullies are calculating in their actions and thrive off the misery of others, which feeds the personality of the bully's soul and becomes an addictive behavior for some. It's like an adrenaline rush with instantaneous gratification that gives them that feel-good exhilarating feeling. Many bullies strategically spend time planning their emotional and/or physical attacks. Other people, events, interests, etc. in their life are pushed to the wayside for they, at times, get so consumed in their creative and devious planning that they become oblivious to their surroundings. For some, bullying becomes a way of life, providing an escape for the individual from their environment, and for many, a means of survival.

TAKING BACK YOUR LIFE

How do you escape the clutches of a bully and regain control of your life?

You defuse the bomb and snuff out the flames. A bully has no power over you if you don't let them. You are in control. You have the power. Make your voice be heard. Tell them to stop, and tell your parents, tell your teachers, tell the school counselor, tell someone with authority. Pull yourself out from under the influence and abuse of a bully and take back your life.

In short, defuse the bully and snuff out the control.

CONCLUSION

Bullying exists everywhere in every country. There's no way to escape it. You can try to stop it in its tracks, contain and control it, and provide the necessary tools to keep from fostering more bullies—through educating and making everyone aware there are different forms of bullying and offering the tools needed to help and heal the victims and the tools needed to identifying a bully and getting the bully the help they so desperately need.

Bullying is a cry for help, and everyone's cry may be for different reasons, but nonetheless it is a cry for help. Get them the help they so desperately need. Heal the victims and the bullies from within. Help stop the violence in our schools and on our playgrounds. Protect our children. For the bullies we cultivate and ignore in the present will only become adult monsters whom we will fear even more so in the future.

AUTHOR BIO

Michelle Barbieri is an author and businesswoman. Most importantly, she is a loving mother to two inspirational boys. As a young child, Michelle was abused verbally and physically. She knew that abuse was not what life had intended for anyone and was not acceptable. In adulthood, her continued experiences with bullying in different relationships continued to teach her new lessons she never thought she would need to learn. In each case, Michelle found the inner strength to escape the clutches of life's different bullies. Michelle isn't a trained psychologist, but the accumulative years of having experienced the different means of being bullied, has provided her with great insight and the knowledge into not only the world of the victim and survivor but the world of the bully as well. Through these experiences she hopes to use her books to change lives.